MW01441329

BIRDS CAN FLY AND A FLY GOES BUZZ
TRICKY, STICKY WORDS

By STEPHEN O'CONOR
Illustrations by ANNABEL TEMPEST
Music by MARK OBLINGER

CANTATA LEARNING

WWW.CANTATALEARNING.COM

CANTATA LEARNING

Published by Cantata Learning
1710 Roe Crest Drive
North Mankato, MN 56003
www.cantatalearning.com

Copyright © 2018 Cantata Learning

All rights reserved. No part of this publication may be reproduced
in any form without written permission from the publisher.

A note to educators and librarians from the publisher: Cantata Learning has provided the following data to assist in book processing and suggested use of Cantata Learning product.

Publisher's Cataloging-in-Publication Data
Prepared by Librarian Consultant: Ann-Marie Begnaud
Library of Congress Control Number: 2016938083
    Birds Can Fly and a Fly Goes Buzz : Tricky, Sticky Words
    Series: Read, Sing, Learn
    By Stephen O'Conor
    Illustrations by Annabel Tempest
    Music by Mark Oblinger
    Summary: Learn about homonyms, words that are spelled the same but have different meanings, in this playful song.
    ISBN: 978-1-63290-795-0 (library binding/CD)
Suggested Dewey and Subject Headings:
    Dewey: E 428.1
    LCSH Subject Headings: Homonyms – Juvenile literature. | Animals – Juvenile literature. | Homonyms – Songs and music – Texts. | Animals – Songs and music – Texts. | Homonyms – Juvenile sound recordings. | Animals – Juvenile sound recordings.
    Sears Subject Headings: English language – homonyms. | Animals. | School songbooks. | Children's songs. | Jazz music.
    BISAC Subject Headings: JUVENILE NONFICTION / Language Arts / Vocabulary & Spelling. | JUVENILE NONFICTION / Music / Songbooks. | JUVENILE NONFICTION / Animals / General.

Book design and art direction: Tim Palin Creative
Editorial direction: Flat Sole Studio
Music direction: Elizabeth Draper
Music written and produced by Mark Oblinger

Printed in the United States of America in North Mankato, Minnesota.
0/2017   0367CGF17

ACCESS THE MUSIC!
SCAN CODE WITH MOBILE APP
CANTATALEARNING.COM

TIPS TO SUPPORT LITERACY AT HOME

WHY READING AND SINGING WITH YOUR CHILD IS SO IMPORTANT

Daily reading with your child leads to increased academic achievement. Music and songs, specifically rhyming songs, are a fun and easy way to build early literacy and language development. Music skills correlate significantly with both phonological awareness and reading development. Singing helps build vocabulary and speech development. And reading and appreciating music together is a wonderful way to strengthen your relationship.

READ AND SING EVERY DAY!

TIPS FOR USING CANTATA LEARNING BOOKS AND SONGS DURING YOUR DAILY STORY TIME

1. As you sing and read, point out the different words on the page that rhyme. Suggest other words that rhyme.

2. Memorize simple rhymes such as Itsy Bitsy Spider and sing them together. This encourages comprehension skills and early literacy skills.

3. Use the questions in the back of each book to guide your singing and storytelling.

4. Read the included sheet music with your child while you listen to the song. How do the music notes correlate to the words of the song?

5. Sing along on the go and at home. Access music by scanning the QR code on each Cantata book. You can also stream or download the music for free to your computer, smartphone, or mobile device.

Devoting time to daily reading shows that you are available for your child. Together, you are building language, literacy, and listening skills.

Have fun reading and singing!

What comes to mind when you hear the word *bark*? Do you think of a dog's bark or the bark on a tree? Either way, you are correct! These words are homonyms. They are spelled the same but have different meanings.

Are there other tricky, sticky words? Find out by turning the page. Remember to sing along!

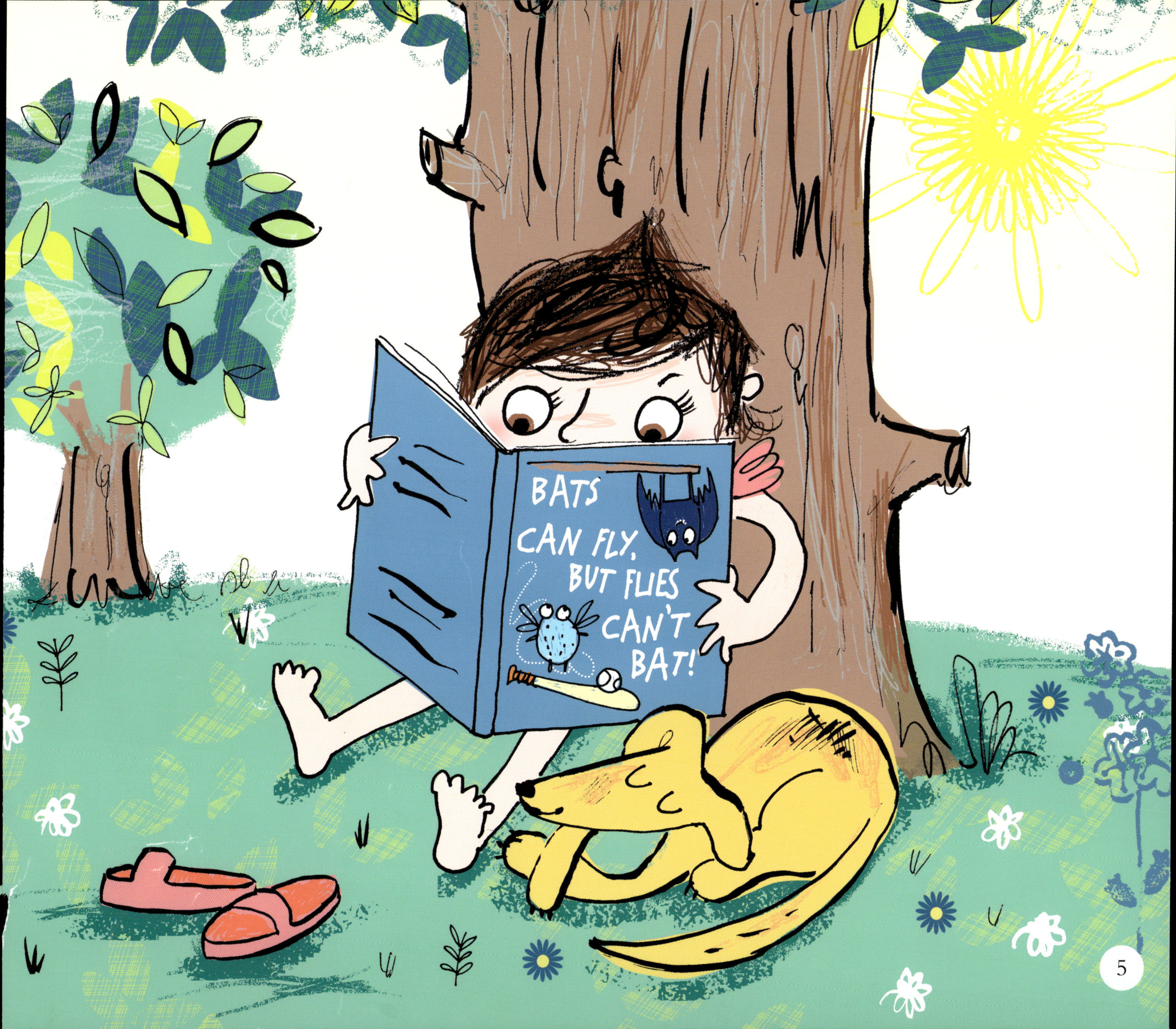
BATS
CAN FLY,
BUT FLIES
CAN'T
BAT!

Funny, funny animal words,
oh, that's the song we sing.

When you hear the word *bark*,
what does *bark* mean?

One little word can mean many, many things.

Funny, funny animal words, oh, that's the song we sing.

Does *bark* mean the sound
a dog makes when running free?

Or does *bark* mean the rough
and woody skin of a tree?

Bark is a funny word.

Remember, if you choose it.

A dog can bark.

A tree has bark.

It depends on how you use it!

Funny, funny animal words,
oh, that's the song we sing.

When you hear the word *fly*,
what does *fly* mean?

One little word can mean many, many things.

Funny, funny animal words, oh, that's the song we sing.

Does *fly* mean a buzzing bug with wings and buggy eyes?

Or does *fly* mean when a bird or kite soars through the skies?

Fly is a funny word.

Remember, if you choose it.

Birds can fly.

A fly goes, "Buzz."

It depends on how you use it!

Funny, funny animal words,
oh, that's the song we sing.

When you hear the word *duck*,
what does *duck* mean?

One little word can mean many, many things.

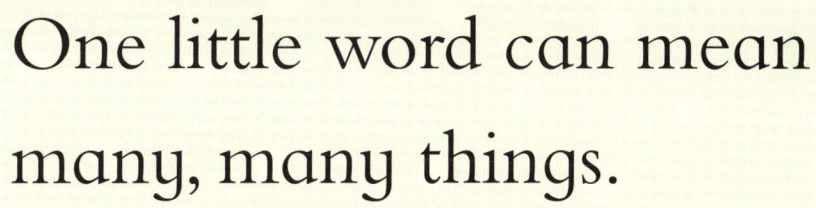

Funny, funny animal words, oh, that's the song we sing.

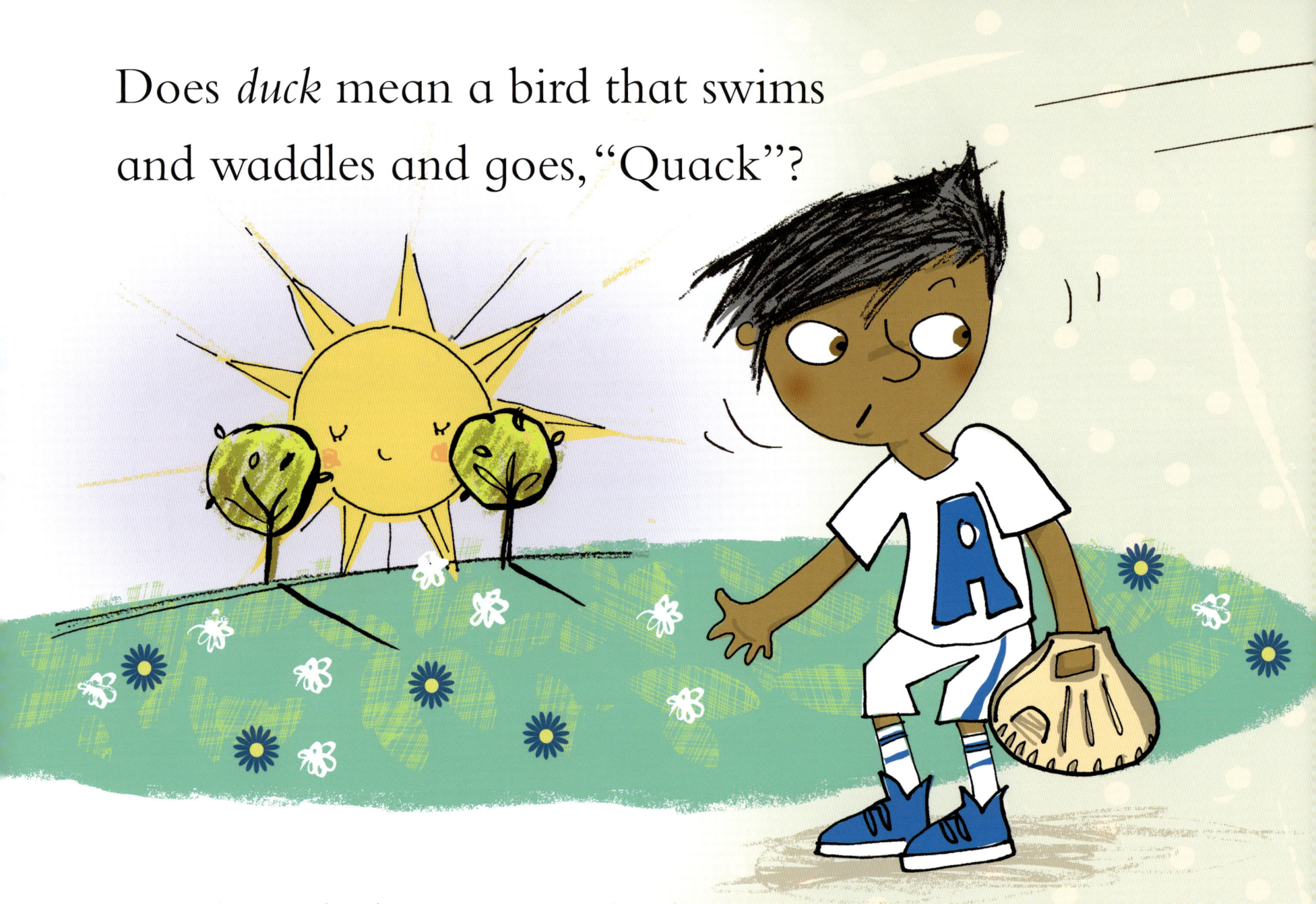

Does *duck* mean a bird that swims and waddles and goes, "Quack"?

Or does *duck* mean to duck down low when that baseball bat goes "whack"?

Duck is a funny word.
Remember, if you choose it.

You can duck down low.
A duck can quack.

It depends on how you use it!

Funny, funny animal words,
oh, that's the song we sing.

When you hear the word *bat*,
what does *bat* mean?

One little word can mean many, many things.

Funny, funny animal words, oh, that's the song we sing.

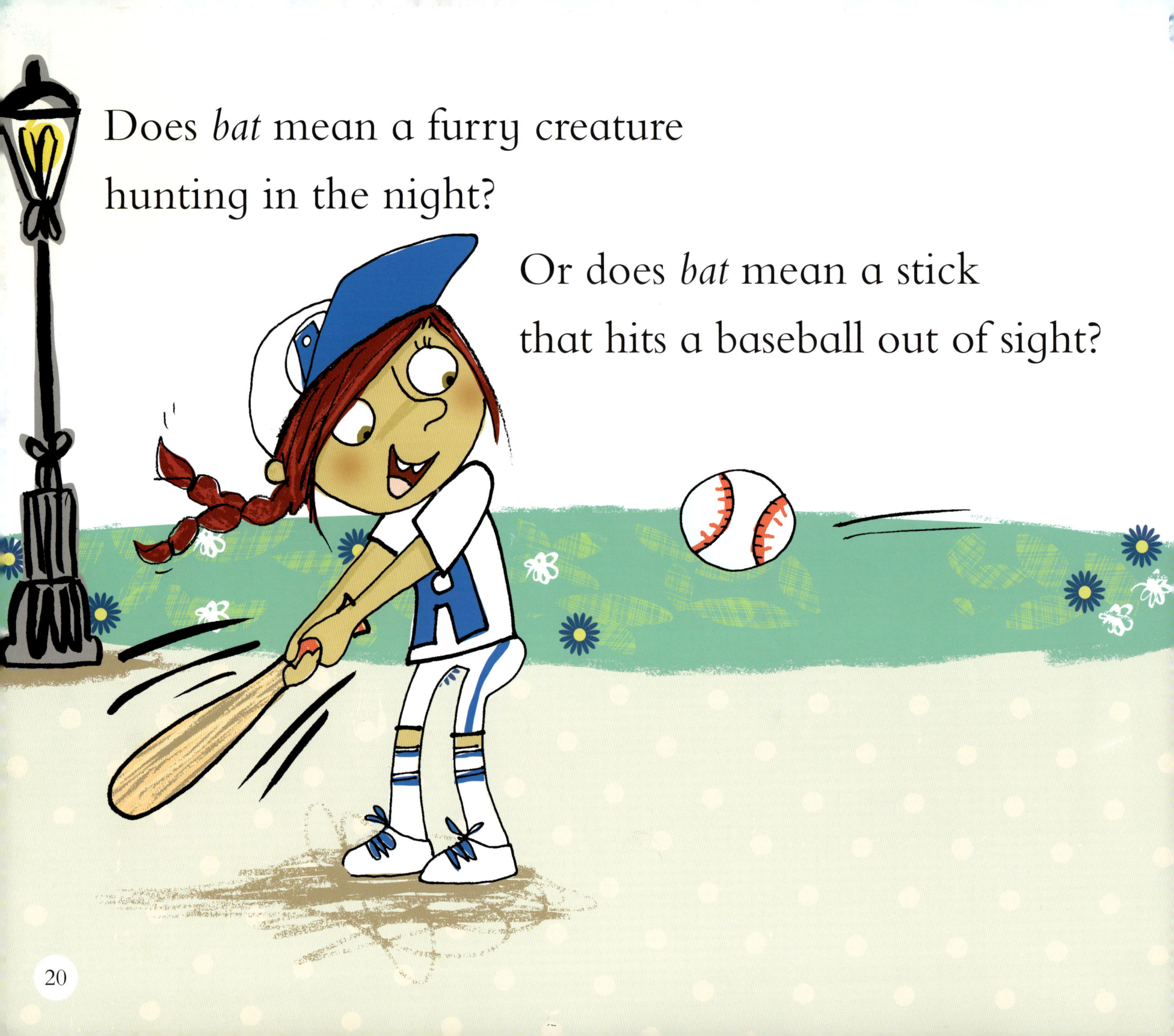

Does *bat* mean a furry creature hunting in the night?

Or does *bat* mean a stick that hits a baseball out of sight?

Bat is a funny word.
Remember, if you choose it.

The bat can hang.
You can hit with a bat.

It depends on how you use it!

Funny, funny animal words,
oh, that's the song we sing.

SONG LYRICS
Birds Can Fly and a Fly Goes Buzz

Funny, funny animal words,
oh, that's the song we sing.
When you hear the word bark,
what does bark mean?

One little word can mean
many, many things.
Funny, funny animal words,
oh, that's the song we sing.

Does bark mean the sound
a dog makes when running free?
Or does bark mean the rough
and woody skin of a tree?

Bark is a funny word.
Remember, if you choose it.
A dog can bark.
A tree has bark.
It depends on how you use it!

Funny, funny animal words,
oh, that's the song we sing.
When you hear the word fly,
what does fly mean?

One little word can mean
many, many things.
Funny, funny animal words,
oh, that's the song we sing.

Does fly mean a buzzing bug
with wings and buggy eyes?
Or does fly mean when a bird
or kite soars through the skies?

Fly is a funny word.
Remember, if you choose it.
Birds can fly.
A fly goes, "Buzz."
It depends on how you use it!

Funny, funny animal words,
oh, that's the song we sing.
When you hear the word duck,
what does duck mean?

One little word can mean
many, many things.
Funny, funny animal words,
oh, that's the song we sing.

Does duck mean a bird that swims
and waddles and goes, "Quack"?
Or does duck mean to duck
down low when that baseball bat goes
   "whack"?

Duck is a funny word.
Remember, if you choose it.
You can duck down low.
A duck can quack.
It depends on how you use it!

Funny, funny animal words,
oh, that's the song we sing.
When you hear the word bat,
what does bat mean?

One little word can mean
many, many things.
Funny, funny animal words,
oh, that's the song we sing.

Does bat mean a furry creature
hunting in the night?
Or does bat mean a stick that hits
a baseball out of sight?

Bat is a funny word.
Remember, if you choose it.
The bat can hang.
You can hit with a bat.
It depends on how you use it!

Funny, funny animal words,
oh, that's the song we sing.

Birds Can Fly and a Fly Goes Buzz

Jazz
Mark Oblinger

Verse

1. Fun-ny, fun-ny an-i-mal words, oh, that's the song we sing. When you hear the word bark, what does bark mean? One lit-tle word can mean man-y, man-y things. Fun-ny, fun-ny an-i-mal words, oh, that's the song we sing. Does bark mean the sound a dog makes when run-ning free? Or does bark mean the rough and wood-y skin of a tree? Bark is a fun-ny word. Re-mem-ber, if you choose it. A dog can bark. A tree has bark. It de-pends on how you use it!

Verse 2
Funny, funny animal words, oh, that's the song we sing.
When you hear the word fly, what does fly mean?
One little word can mean many, many things.
Funny, funny animal words, oh, that's the song we sing.

Does fly mean a buzzing bug with wings and buggy eyes?
Or does fly mean when a bird or kite soars through the skies?
Fly is a funny word. Remember, if you choose it.
Birds can fly. A fly goes, "Buzz." It depends on how you use it!

Verse 3
Funny, funny animal words, oh, that's the song we sing.
When you hear the word duck, what does duck mean?
One little word can mean many, many things.
Funny, funny animal words, oh, that's the song we sing.

Does duck mean a bird that swims and waddles and goes, "Quack"?
Or does duck mean to duck down low when that baseball bat goes "whack"?
Duck is a funny word. Remember, if you choose it.
You can duck down low. A duck can quack. It depends on how you use it!

Verse 4
Funny, funny animal words, oh, that's the song we sing.
When you hear the word bat, what does bat mean?
One little word can mean many, many things.
Funny, funny animal words, oh, that's the song we sing.

Does bat mean a furry creature hunting in the night?
Or does bat mean a stick that hits a baseball out of sight?
Bat is a funny word. Remember, if you choose it.
The bat can hang. You can hit with a bat. It depends on how you use it!

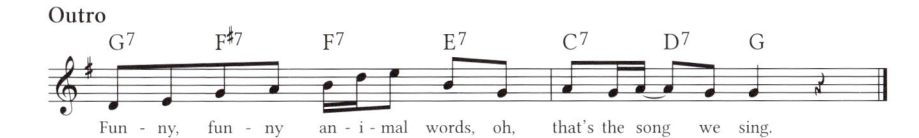

Outro

Fun-ny, fun-ny an-i-mal words, oh, that's the song we sing.

GLOSSARY

Homonyms

bark—the sound a dog makes

bark—the rough outside layer of a tree

bat—a furry animal that flies at night

bat—the stick used to hit a baseball

duck—a swimming bird

duck—to squat and bend your head down

fly—a buzzing insect

fly—to go through the air like a bird

GUIDED READING ACTIVITIES

1. Homonyms are words that can have more than one meaning. What are two meanings for the words *box*, *rose*, *tire*, and *wave*?

2. Pick one of the homonyms from this song. Draw a picture that shows both meanings of the word.

3. Listen to this song with a friend. Every time you hear the word *bark*, one of you barks like a dog and the other stands tall like a tree. Now make up moves for the words *bat*, *duck*, and *fly*.

TO LEARN MORE

Anderson, Steven. *Five Little Ducks*. North Mankato, MN: Cantata Learning, 2016.

Cleary, Brian P. *A Bat Cannot Bat, a Stair Cannot Stare: More about Homonyms and Homophones*. Minneapolis: Millbrook, 2014.

Felix, Rebecca. *Can You Be a Bee?* Mankato, MN: Amicus, 2015.

Johnson, Angelique J. *Bats*. North Mankato, MN: Capstone, 2011.